Praise for Industrial Oz

Industrial Oz may just be the most cogent and sustained collection of quality eco-activist poetry ever written in this culture, this country. I know of no other that has such clear focus and such wide-ranging inclusiveness. In concise poems that have the reflective essence of ancient Oriental haiku, Scott Starbuck is a modern-day Han-shan; a Che Guevara of the literary environmental movement; a true bardic poet and town-crier. Like the ghost of Paul Revere riding through the pages of America's streets he cries out to all of us: "extinction is forever." And in his poem "Otter Log" he writes: "After otters were extinct...children drew otters/in schools.../asking why we lost them/and what was more important/than having them here." Amen and Amen!
— Thomas Rain Crowe, Publisher of New Native Press

"Are You Really Awake?" asks a bumper sticker in an early poem. After reading these poems, you will be. These powerful poems of protest traverse the insanities of our world, from war to corporate power to climate change, elegantly implicating us all. Subtly charged, laced with humor and surprising connections, they reveal the absurdity of destruction in all its guises. Here, dreamscapes and reality merge, creating the light by which we might find a new path, one in which we choose, as a war veteran says, "mindfulness/instead of a grenade." This is a vital and necessary work.
— Marybeth Holleman, 8th World Wilderness Congress Poetry Award and author of *The Heart of the Sound: An Alaskan Paradise Found and Nearly Lost*

Industrial Oz

Ecopoems

Scott T. Starbuck

Fomite
Burlington, VT

Copyright © 2015 by Scott T. Starbuck

All rights reserved. No part of this book may be reproduced in any form or by any means without the prior written consent of the publisher, except in the case of brief quotations used in reviews and certain other noncommercial uses permitted by copyright law.

Scott T. Starbuck will donate 30% of his 80% royalty to 350.org's global climate movement that has successfully challenged systems leading to catastrophic climate change, and is acting for a more just and sustainable future.

ISBN-13: 978-1-942515-16-6

Library of Congress Control Number: 2015951033

Cover art Copyright © 2015 by Abigail Kaarla

These poems have been "written to increase the chances of Abigail having a decent life, or a life at all."

Fomite
58 Peru Street
Burlington, VT 05401
www.fomitepress.com

Contents

The Art of Denial	1
Climate Subtext	2
Wasting Sea Stars	3
Bumper Sticker: Extinction is Forever	4
Antarctic Dream After Watching *Chasing Ice*	5
Glacial River Poem	6
Unraveling Has Begun	7
Essex, 1820	8
Meteor	10
Rain Forest Poem	11
Thinking About Global Warming and the Orange Tree Outside My Kitchen Window	12
Global Warming Serpent	13
Wrecking Ball Dream	15
In Oracle, Arizona	16
Listening to Fireworks Near the 2014 FOR Seabeck Conference	17
Levitating Turtles of Sauvie's Island	18
Speaking to a Street Person About the Problem With North America	19
And They Thought We Were Talking About Caribou	20
Of Whales and the Hinckley Hunt on Christmas Eve, 1818	21
What If One Night a Big Solar Storm Went By?	22
Poem for Dissolving Sea Stars	25
Reflections in a Garden of Undersea Statues	26
Chorus	27
Smoked Whale, Circa 1987	28
Otter Log	29
Brook Trout	30
Thinking About the Association of Writers & Writing Programs 2014 Conference in Seattle	31
Why All US-Made Nuclear Waste Must Be Stored at the White House	32
Photo Circa 1969, The Art of Redaction	35
At the Nevada Nuclear Test Site	36
Plutonium Fish	37

Through a Wire Fence	38
Erratum	39
Tent Caterpillars	40
How It Is	41
Louisiana Agates	42
Omen Poem	43
Men Wandering Around Alaska Looking for a TV Set	44
The Old One's Letter	45
Moon and Money Poem	46
Listening to a Banker Talk About Losing [Only] Two Billion Dollars as Schools Are Closed	47
San Diego Swap Meet	48
The Dream of Greece, Wisconsin, and One-armed Trees	49
If Washington Were Pompeii	50
Before You Were Born	51
After 2008	52
Patient Y	53
Demon Fish	54
Hiking the Superstition Mountains I Realized	55
The Day I Appeared on TV	56
The Kid at Calico Rock	57
Hiking the Coast Range Mountains	58
Fishing Trip on the Deschutes River in Oregon	59
How to Fish the Wind	60
Reflections on Sand Creek, Colorado	61
People on 17th Street in Portland, Oregon, Dreaming of Dogs	62
View of Modern War from Space Station	63
The Vagrant Says	64
Earth Like the Deck of a Ship	65
What I Can't Say at My Neighbor's Party Looking at a Map of the United States	66
Ode to a Mexican Family	67
Intoxicated by Purple Lupine,	68
Creative Writing Professor as Iron Worker	69
Local History	70
Another Legend of Stonehenge	71
After Two Weeks in Wilderness	72

God Doesn't Show Up at the Rose Festival Parade	73
The Fishes He Caught	74
Enlightenment for $19.99	75
Peter Went Fishing	77
Ancient Sacred Texts Conversing in the Library at Alexandria	78
Poem Against Yellow School Buses	79
Techno Man	80
Unintended Art	81
On the Ferry Between Port Angeles and Victoria	82
Poem for Ishi	83
Houses on Siletz Spit	84
Coyote's Prediction	85
Congress of Fish	86
Big Sur Satori	87
River Reflections	88
At Lake Absarraca	89
Bear-like Tree Shadows on a Dying Chinook Salmon	90
Raft Trip	91
If	92
Octomato Nightmare	93
Saint Arkhipov	95
Instead of Drones, I Dream of Peace Piñatas	97
Advisory	98
Three-Sided Lizard	99
Facts	100
"State OKs money for drone test range in Eastern Oregon" – KATU.com, 3/22/15	101
Salish Sea Prophecy	102
Forget Math and English	103
Snowflake Immortality	104
Acknowledgments	107

"For the reality of politics, we must go to the poets, not to the politicians."
— Norman O. Brown, *Love's Body*, Chapter 1, "Liberty"

The Art of Denial

If you ignore a thorn in your hand
it will go away

but first the hand gets infected, swells,
turns coal-purple,

and sometimes parts must be amputated
to save what remains.

Disease could have been prevented
by simply removing the thorn

but companies that owned it
said no.

Climate Subtext

"Is it ok for scientists to weep over climate change?"
by Roger Harrabin, *The Guardian*, July 9, 2015

Let's scientifically and objectively study
rape of your Mother,

her eyes as breasts are torn,
pitch of her voice

as she repeatedly screams
your name.

Forget nurturing you had
as a child,

baby sparrows
you two discovered.

We'll measure magnitude
of wounds,

erratic pulse,
voice decibels,

even document
names and titles of abusers.

What's not allowed
in our courtroom

of public opinion
is for you to feel anything.

Wasting Sea Stars

Tide pool consciousness means you don't know
about bacteria, viruses, or coal-fired plants
making sea water acidic.

Instead, you focus on gathering
succulent mussels for a dinner
written in your genetic code.

You crawl, mate, leave offspring,
protect your territory
under ledges of barnacled rocks.

And when stars begin to drop around you,
your arms melt and unhinge,
you merely move along as you always have.

Bumper Sticker: Extinction is Forever

Symbolically, a drunk chases a moth with a swatter,
not knowing it has the head of his newborn son.

What I mean is Bach's scores were reportedly used
to wrap meat, and reviewers hated *Moby Dick*.

Few understood the secret codes
or their future importance.

What I mean is all those years I studied,
read, spoke, taught, and watched,

innumerable plants and animals vanished
without you or me raising a finger.

What I mean is right now, as I write this,
that moth's head is yours, and mine, and everyone's.

Antarctic Dream After Watching *Chasing Ice*

The bumper sticker near the airport asks
"Are You Really Awake?"

As I fly south on Alaska Airlines Flight 529,
a kid beside me watches *Gilligan's Island* reruns.

I drift off, and the pilot announces
Amundsen Sea Embayment just melted

so during the trip from Portland to San Diego
the sea will rise 20 feet.

"I guess that wrecks my surf trip," says Gilligan.
"I guess that wrecks my ocean-front condo," says Ginger.

"I guess that wrecks London, Tokyo, Mumbai, New York,
Bangladesh, and the Netherlands," says the Professor.

Glacial River Poem

"Some of Mount Hood's glaciers have lost as much as about 60 percent of their surface area to melting since the early 1900s, according to research by Portland State University scientists." from "A Region's Vitality, Melting Away" by Michael Milstein, *The Oregonian*, February 11, 2008

Without glacial water
there are no apples, pears, or cherries
near Hood River,
no trout, steelhead or salmon in
The Sandy or Clackamas Rivers.

There are no rowboats or campfires
at Olallie or Timothy Lakes,
no skiers or snowboarders
at Timberline or Meadows.

There are no families,
migratory geese, or songs
at Oxbow, Dodge, or McIver Parks.
In short, without glacial water
there is no reason to be here.

Thousands of years of human joy
flowed freely from the ice.

All around the mountain,
bankers, mayors, and sheriffs
believed they were in charge.
They were wrong.
It was the clouds that fed
the glaciers.

Unraveling Has Begun

By July of 2015 Washington trucked salmon
up shallow rivers to spawn,

and 400,000 Columbia River sockeye were thought
to die from heat exhaustion or disease.

Oregon's Willamette River went to 80 °F
killing salmon, steelhead, and sturgeon.

The sky says get ready for more
and worse.

I walked beside dying salmon
flowering gills like wild roses,

prayed for them, for you,
helped if I could.

I recalled Ishi who survived
murder of his tribe,

rethought our blue jewel planet
worn until now

by an oil industry harlot.

Essex, 1820

"An ice sheet in West Antarctica is hemorrhaging a volume of ice equivalent to Mount Everest every two years, a rate much faster than scientists previously thought [. . .]" Zoë Schlanger in *Newsweek* 12/5/14

What were they thinking,
men who drew lots
and chose cannibalism,
after a giant sperm whale
defending his mate,
rammed their now sunken ship?

Did they sing to lift spirits,
and did this remind them
of grief-stricken whales
whose mates they killed,
echoing thousands of undersea miles
under champagned celebrations?

The men's predator spirits
with too many victories
to recall or count
suddenly turned prey
in a tiny lifeboat inside
the horror instead of outside it.

Like proud men of the USA
facing climate destruction
they and their fathers,
without any foresight,
brought on themselves
and their children.

And like that day on the lifeboat,
Hopi elder Dan Evehema said
"The degree of violence will be determined

by the degree of inequity
caused among the peoples of the world
and in the balance of nature." *

"In this crisis rich and poor
will be forced to struggle as equals
in order to survive." *

* Anonymous Hopi

Meteor

I'm in a 6 a.m. Cloud 9 Shuttle in San Diego with blasting radio
and the host describes an early November fireball.
"I thought it was the Big One," says another DJ.

"Imagine if it hit us" offers the driver.

"It already has," I reply. "People just don't know it yet."

It is the day before Typhoon Haiyan will hit the Philippines
leaving four million homeless,
and I'm thinking about declining red knot shorebirds
which sources note, in some areas "could disappear within five years"
due to global warming, which also brings northern migrating viruses,
and moose infested with ticks from British Columbia to Maine
driven crazy as they rub off fur on pines
then die from hypothermia.

The United Nations Environment Programme notes
"Scientists estimate that between 150 and 200 species of life
become extinct every 24 hours [, ...]
the greatest rate of extinction since the vanishing of the dinosaurs"
65 million years ago.

The driver turns the radio down as we wind
through Point Loma hills in silence, which,
as any reflective person knows,
are never really silent.

Rain Forest Poem

One day, the liver complained
to the brain—Hey,
you're poisoning me.

Not my fault, said the brain.
Go talk to the stomach.

I spend hours processing
your food, said the stomach.
Besides, I take orders
from taste buds.

The liver considered.
Listen, it said, if I go
you all go.

We'll see about that
said the rest of the body.

Thinking About Global Warming and the Orange Tree Outside My Kitchen Window

The problem with metaphor is
a painting of an orange
is not an orange.
Humans and birds need to eat.

Real oranges are suspended
like little worlds
on their long branches.

Pacific mist makes them glisten
in the morning
and the noon sun makes them glow.

When I was sick with the flu
my landlord brought me some
to drink.

Sometimes they fall,
turn orange-yellow
then red as Mars and rot.

Birds harvest insects
and seeds
make new sprouts.

The problem with metaphor is
a poem about the Earth
is not the Earth.

Global Warming Serpent

"Study: California Drought Most Severe Dry Spell in at least 1,200 Years"
— Alex Emslie in *KQED Science*, 12/4/14

Soon, there will be no
rain on a dry riverbed
or wild jasmine in summer.

Together we shall desecrate land
as sex-starved soldiers
desecrate virgins.

In my name
we will kill circles, songs, light,
feet, voices, trees, rivers,

children, parents, lovers
and, most of all,
capacity to resist.

We will corrupt the Nile,
Amazon, Yangtze, Mississippi,
Ob, Yenisei, Yellow River,

Congo, Amur, Parana,
Lena, Mackenzie, Niger,
Mekong, Volga, Murray-Darling,

and Rio-Grande.
Glaciers will melt.
Groundwater will be fracked

until pure water costs more than gas.
There will be no end
until permanent damage is done

to the blue gem you call home.
Do you doubt me?
Does sky have nerve endings?

Can your rock breathe?

Wrecking Ball Dream

Without warning
half the roof is gone

but poker players
are drunk on winning.

Even when one is hit
and drops

the game continues
until another is gone,

and another,
and another.

Finally, the American,
alone in his chair,

refuses to even look
at raging sea.

In Oracle, Arizona

The engineer says his company's
50 thousand dollar computer
has an outdoor sensor
that can tell moon phase,
weather, and season.

It has an indestructible Webcam
disguised as a cactus
remotely activated
from up to two miles.

I laugh because I can step outside
under the stars and look.
He stares at his shiny Mephistos,
"For now, you can."
"Meaning what?" I ask.

He says if I have to ask,
I need the computer.

Listening to Fireworks Near the 2014 FOR Seabeck Conference

for Gary Snyder

The real work
is daily practice
in order to be
of greater service.

Skies are filled
with vibrant explosions,
oohs and aahs
while the truth

like a cedar raven
waits and speaks
at in-between
silence.

Levitating Turtles of Sauvie's Island

"I'm waiting," I say.

"Hush," she says,

adding these beasts
are like poems

and never fly
if you directly look.

Somewhere across
the river

fireworks are starting
which I also don't believe.

Speaking to a Street Person
About the Problem With North America

If the world is a house on fire
there is a room upstairs
where a party rages, music plays,
beautiful men and women
dance and drink the night away

right up to smoke entering
through door cracks
and no one can hear sirens
because music and laughter
are too loud for all
except us dogs to hear.

And They Thought We Were Talking About Caribou

In the dream geologists report there is a 95% chance
of drilling 16 billion barrels of dinosaur blood
from the Arctic National Wildlife Refuge,
the land Gwich'in hunters call
"the sacred place where life begins."

So we drill and destabilize Earth's rotation.

Next, there is a massive pole shift.
The Pacific Ocean flows into Phoenix, Arizona.
So the Phoenix legend continues its circular story
until separateness is recognized as illusion
by some future remnant of humans.

Of Whales and the Hinckley Hunt on Christmas Eve, 1818

"An 1890 engraving depicts the Great Hinckley Hunt of 1818. Nearly 600 men participated in the Christmas Eve hunt, which bagged 21 bears, 17 wolves, 300 deer and untold numbers of turkeys, foxes and raccoons."
—Mark J. Price, *Beacon Journal*, December 22, 2013

The spring after the 1818 massacre of corralled Ohio wildlife
there were no wolf howls under a full moon,

no red fox flashes at dawn,
no pesky bears harming fences and livestock.

With predators gone and deer out of fields,
farmers had a better chance of survival.

It was reported they sang, told stories,
and filled bellies with game.

It was a different world then
with different pressures and habits

like how my ancestors, 800 miles east,
shipped out to kill sperm whales,

risking huge toothy jaws
that killed or crippled thousands.

The Treaty of St. Mary's had been signed in October
dooming the Myaaniaki Tribe to Oklahoma territory

and Christ child was safe in manger.
Bear and whale fat dripped off hair and faces.

Buzzards gathered.
Chickens and sheep would be safe.

What If One Night a Big Solar Storm Went By?

"Analysts believe that a direct hit by an extreme CME [coronal mass ejection] such as the one that missed Earth in July 2012 could cause widespread power blackouts, disabling everything that plugs into a wall socket. Most people wouldn't even be able to flush their toilet because urban water supplies largely rely on electric pumps. [. . . .] [It could have sent] modern civilization back to the 18th century."
—Dr. Tony Phillips, *Science@NASA,* July 23, 2014

Imagine everyone forgot language
so that no one could argue, buy, sell, cheat or lie.

All computer hard drives were wiped clean
and circuits didn't work anyway.

Starbucks, GM, GE, and BP were gibberish.
War, cars, radio, and TV were impossible.

Libraries were shelves of paperweights.
Laws and regulations were void.

Google faded out of consciousness
along with cell phones

and people began to mistake
fork-like cell towers for modern art.

Money, billboards, and sacred texts meant nothing.
Constellations guided travelers.

Terrified and speechless,
Congress and the President just sat and stared.

But sky appeared as always.
Geese, whales, caribou and salmon migrated.

Cougars hunted in forests
and bears ate meadow berries.

Suddenly, men had to listen in wordless ways
to women, stars, seasons, and each other.

People had vague memories of who they were
and where they had been before the storm

but no one could read names, titles, maps, or road signs
even though comics

and spontaneity of dogs, cats, and children
still made them laugh.

Like after an Ice Age without ice,
everyone had to learn from scratch.

People noticed colors, sounds, and smells
outside in ways they never had.

Pine trees, like in pioneer times, became close friends.
Humans who hadn't smiled in years smiled.

People rose at sunrise
and went to bed at moonrise.

The wheel and sewing needle
became essential.

Doctors had to relearn doctoring.
Parents had to relearn parenting.

Farmers had to relearn farming.
Builders had to relearn building.

Cooks had to relearn cooking.
You get the idea.

Somehow artists and musicians
made art and music but,

because no one could read names,
their fame was limited to locals.

It was mostly unknown when
San Andreas Fault slid LA into the Pacific

and another tsunami took out
the top half of Japan.

When Mount St. Helens made Seattle
look like Pompeii

there were no advertisers, merchants
or media to profit.

The human mind changed in ways
that had been impossible.

Without countless pressures, distractions,
clogged airways, and moving images in boxes

people began to hear themselves
in green and blue silences

so that Taoist monks and tai chi
became the norm.

It was the worst time ever
for bankers and politicians

and the best time for everyone else.

Poem for Dissolving Sea Stars

Four months before bulldozers destroyed the forest
behind my Oregon house, salamanders, crawfish, pheasants,
and owls pleaded in dreams for me to save them.
I couldn't do anything but write a letter
to the City of Tigard from my twelve-year-old hand . It failed.

In 1974 everything was falling apart. My parents divorced.
A soccer stampede in Cairo killed 49 people.
A World War II Japanese holdout emerged.
In less than 24 hours, 148 tornadoes killed 319 people
from Illinois to North Carolina.
Patty Hearst and her M1 carbine robbed a bank in San Francisco.

What could it all mean? Later in a library, searching to understand,
I read an astrophysics book in which the author explained Earth
made a massive investment in humans because it would only be us
who would carry Her life to the cosmos
before our aged oscillating sun destroyed everything.

On April 13, 2014, Justin Gillis of *The New York Times* reported
in "Climate Efforts Falling Short, U.N. Panel Says,"
"a rise of 2 degrees Celsius above the preindustrial level"
may mean "a rapid rise in sea levels,
difficulty growing enough food, huge die-offs of forests,
and mass extinctions of plant and animal species."
November 30, 2013, NBCNews.com reported
"an epidemic [is] killing millions of starfish."
It's not the first starfish die-off, but it is the worst.

Walking along La Jolla Cove, I saw them clinging to rocks
like brain neurons that won't let go of believing,
like sawed-off hands of clowns, still laughing as they moved
in all their vibrant colors.

Reflections in a Garden of Undersea Statues

We hoped the storm wouldn't find us,
thundering through disturbed corals
and sea surface,

hands wouldn't bleed like others
too close to the road
or on the wrong side of the fence.

Frozen, we posed, eyes deep in the forest,
holding a breast or an apple,
dreaming of faraway paradise,

waiting for an external flute
to put everything in motion.

Chorus

Not for an ocean floor
of drowned polar bear cubs
will I give up my car.

Not for a sky
without a single bird
for a hundred thousand miles.

Not for my children,
grandchildren,
or great great grandchildren.

Not to stop drought
from Haiti to Houston
or Fairbanks to the Falkland Islands.

If God didn't want us
to drive cars,
why did He make them?

Smoked Whale, Circa 1987

Sickly sweet wood smoke wafts
over the central Oregon coast
as three gray whales breathe it in
and dive deep.

I call the Oregon Dept. of Environmental Quality
on the whales' behalf.
"Is this a crank call?" someone asks.
"Are you a crank?" I ask.

"Well, what do you want
me to do about it?"
I tell her to prohibit slash burning
on days with east wind,

fill her lungs with wood smoke
and retrieve a quarter
from the bottom of the river.

Otter Log

After otters were extinct
they showed up
as faces in rock formations
or body shapes diving in logs.

A young man thought
he saw one
in the harbor
but it was just a skipping stone.

Children drew otters
in schools
and noticed
in river shadows,

asking why we lost them
and what was more important
than having them here.

Brook Trout

in fall colors of green, red, and yellow
in Lake Owen in Medicine Bow Forest
are infinitely more beautiful
than any man-made logo.

When I catch one I admire her
in stunned silence
then gently return her sleek form
with wet hands to the lake.

Once, I killed some
mercifully quick with a stone
and watched their colors flee
from quivering dead ripples
back into night forest,
red sky, yellow wildflowers.

Thinking About the Association of Writers & Writing Programs 2014 Conference in Seattle

As poets and story tellers met, sea stars melted unexplainably
along the waterfront from Sitka, Alaska to San Diego.

As presenters spoke, about half of polar bear cubs drowned from having to swim
too far to keep up with their mothers due to global warming.

As the Washington State Convention Center & Sheraton Hotel filled
each morning and emptied each night in a tide of aspiring writers,

Fukushima had its worst spill of radiation in six months,
and California experienced its worst drought since the 1500s.

Professors, directors, and students of the AWP tribe taught
and learned as those before had thousands of years

and hopefully would for thousands more
like a kid with a stick on the Olympic Peninsula,

a writer in his youth, running circles and
delightedly carving sand for onlookers to enjoy

before the next set of waves erased everything.

Why All US-Made Nuclear Waste Must Be Stored at the White House

"The problem is how to keep radioactive waste in storage until it decays after hundreds of thousands of years. The geologic deposit must be absolutely reliable as the quantities of poison are tremendous. It is very difficult to satisfy these requirements for the simple reason that we have had no practical experience with such a long term project. Moreover permanently guarded storage requires a society with unprecedented stability."
—Hannes Alfvené, Nobel laureate in physics, quoted in John Abbotts' October 1979 paper "Radioactive waste: A technical solution?," *Bulletin of the Atomic Scientists*: 12-18.

"Adequately managing these radioactive wastes for 240,000 years is, at best, a daunting proposition. The nuclear industry has already proven itself incapable of keeping track of its high-level nuclear waste for even 30 years. High-level radioactive waste has already gone missing from one, if not several, nuclear reactors."
—greenpeace.org

"I am an FBI agent. My superiors have ordered me to lie about a criminal investigation I headed in 1989. We were investigating the US Department of Energy, but the US Justice Department covered up the truth. I have refused to follow the orders to lie about what really happened during that criminal investigation at Rocky Flats Nuclear Weapons Plant."
— Special Agent Lipsky quoted in *The Ambushed Grand Jury: How the Justice Department Covered up Government Nuclear Crimes and How We Caught Them Red Handed* by Wes McKinley and Caron Balkany

"As a physician, I contend that nuclear technology threatens life on our planet with extinction. All of us will be affected by radioactive contamination, unless we bring about a drastic reversal of our government's pro-nuclear policy."
—Helen Caldicott, MD, at helencaldicott.com

Nobody sane wants it,
not Carlsbad, New Mexico, people,
not Hanford, Washington, people,
not Idaho Falls, Idaho, people,
not Needles, California, people,
not Paducah, Kentucky, people,
not Panhandle, Texas, people,
not Rocky Flats, Colorado, people,
not Savannah River, South Carolina, people,
especially not Yucca Mountain, Nevada, people.

Let those who benefit most
from defense contracts
have it all.

Immediately.
Today.

Eisenhower, in his farewell address,
spoke truth
about dangers
of the military-industrial complex,
but to whom? Sparrows?

His words were recorded
by reporters
and microfiched in libraries.

I saw a film praising
the two-time president and five-star general
for his courage to speak
and thought it ridiculous.

Give the guy credit for D-Day,
but his farewell address was like
if Jesus had said at Gethsemane,
"Father, instead of being crucified,

I just say Satan is bad, okay?"

Eisenhower's conscience, like Oppenheimer's
and ours, is a dreaded glowing
that can never be buried deep enough
to avoid leaching into groundwater.

Photo Circa 1969, The Art of Redaction

That day fishing Eagle Creek
after you returned from Vietnam --
from what the world means,
what it is,
what it does

you longed for
a spring day
when you were 7
and had it in you
to flash a peace sign
to a girl
from the back
of a yellow bus.

On the truck ride home
you said to me,
a truant riding shotgun,
"Overseas, where
the half-drowned
saved the drowning,
you could learn a lot
from Asian people
you didn't bomb."

At the Nevada Nuclear Test Site

grandmothers
are arrested,
imprisoned
      to make way
      for the blast.

A sheriff explains
      the old women
      are dangerous.

Plutonium Fish

Once, high above the polluted river,
sky helped water return
to its natural state.
If left alone long enough
it would come alive again
with purple-sided trout,
a green and yellow choir of frogs,
human families touching
with hands, arms, and words.

Winter didn't have to wait
half a million years for spring.

Through a Wire Fence

I watch boys pull wings
off monarch butterflies
who have just arrived
from distant lands
across the sea.

"She loves me NOT,"
the tallest screeches,
depetaling an orange,
black, and gold wing
then releasing it
to the wind.

The other boys laugh
as the one-winger
spins in circles
on hot pavement
thinking of what?

And the scary part is
later, these boys will
go to the big church,
sing hymns, father sons.

Erratum

I'm sorry
cave paintings at Altamira,
palm-sized Venus of Willendorfs
were so misunderstood
(or deliberately covered up)
by great grandsons.

Most of us never intended
gray breakdown
of our blue jewel,
silencing steel jaws,
but you in cages know
how things begin to fade

when you stop
singing your own songs.

Tent Caterpillars

remind me of human overpopulation
making skeleton trees,
filling roads,
appearing everywhere you don't want them

but still, I am merciful
by watching my step
and cautioning my lover
to do the same.

Finding one in my visor
far from his territory
I had no choice but to squash him
lest his kind infest

orchards across the Salish Sea.
The truth is
I hope we don't discover
a way out of our galaxy

anytime soon
until we're in balance
with every green thing
that breathes or moves.

How It Is

"For several days this month, Greenland's surface ice cover melted over a larger area than at any time in more than 30 years of satellite observations."
—Maria-Joseé Vinñas, *NASA's Earth Science News Team*, July 24, 2012, at www.nasa.gov/topics/earth/features/greenland-melt.html

Sometimes you forget Greenland exists
like two pages stuck together in a novel
or a speed sign missed on a dark highway.

Then it melts and Holland disappears.
At this point everyone wonders,
"Will humanity survive?"

and I think of Butterfield Concrete Company
when I was a boy, and how,
even in harshest neighborhoods

with metal bars on windows,
words in sidewalks were mostly about love.

Louisiana Agates

"[…] federal investigators are also looking into whether several BP engineers involved in drilling the well provided false information to regulators about the risks associated with the project while drilling was in progress."
— "First Criminal Case in Spill" by Tom Fowler, *The Wall Street Journal* [online] U. S. NEWS, April 24, 2012, 7:30 p.m. ET, Ángel González contributed to this article.

"At a federal hearing in May, Mark Hafle said under oath that BP was confident about the safeguards on its Gulf well. But in an e-mail sent on April 14, six days before the deadly explosion aboard the Deepwater Horizon drilling platform, Hafle was the opposite of confident. He called the Macondo well sitting a mile below the ocean's surface "a crazy well." Brian Morel, another drilling engineer who worked with Hafle, described Macondo to colleagues as a "nightmare well which has everyone all over the place." […] BP declined Wednesday to comment on the e-mails. […] Waxman said the congressional investigation alleges that BP took a cost-cutting and speedy approach to drilling the troubled well. […] The letter - co-signed by Oversight and Investigations Subcommittee Chairman Bart Stupak, D-Michigan - asserts that BP saved $10 million in part by skimping on a process to properly cement the well."
— "BP e-mails on well safety don't jibe with engineer's testimony" by the *CNN Wire Staff*, cnn.com, June 16, 2010 3:49 p.m. EDT

In burgundy, ruby, and moss
they glow like pieces of broken sun
or rock candy
featuring ships in bottles,
crawfish, shrimp, oysters,
dolphins, sea turtles,
manatees, leaping fish,
and human faces—
all things that,
minus lies of BP,
could still be today.

Omen Poem

The hawk I saw
north of Santa Barbara
flew higher than oil rigs
offshore.

Men Wandering Around Alaska Looking for a TV Set

"What you got here?"
the newcomers demand,
tired and angry,
unplanned landing.

The Old One smiles again.
He says —
we got plenty of fish
and plenty of friends.

He says — Look
by the river.
We have raven.
The Spruce. The Moon.

Sea is quiet.
Stay if you wish
and tell us
what *you* got.

The Old One's Letter

Here a second can seem so long
like when reaching for a fish with a net.

Other times, ten years goes by
in the blink of a love-struck eye.

I read that Inuit maps are based on "sleeps"
and difficulty of travel.

Before leaving, you must understand
the machine understands none of this.

Moon and Money Poem

Holding up a dollar, I ask the class what it is.

"Freedom," says a Tijuana student,
"from working in a maquiladora."

"Red money," says a San Diego student,
"if you see past the green."

"Cat food." "College." "A cheap prostitute."

I tell them to dig deeper.

"Paper and green ink."

Deeper.

"Dead trees and petroleum."

Imagine you are on the moon
and dig way deeper.

"Symbolism that represents
interests of the symbol-makers."

Good.

I ask who the symbol-makers are
but no one answers.

Flipping the bill,
I end with four treasonous questions:
"Who commissioned this pyramid?"
"Who built it?"
"Barring wages, what was promised
and actually paid?"

Listening to a Banker Talk About Losing [Only] Two Billion Dollars as Schools Are Closed

"Yes, JPMorgan Chase lost $2 billion in late April-early May trading. But last year, this bank earned $17.45 billion."
—Rich Smith, *The Motley Fool*, posted at *Daily Finance* on May 16, 2012

It was a fish with the head of a lion
or maybe it was a goat's head
or maybe it was the head of a rhinoceros.
It's hard to say.
But it had fins, I'm sure of that.
So on Tuesday it was a fish.
By Wednesday, maybe it wasn't a fish.
These fish are like that.
By then, it only looked like a fish.
Like maybe, I only look like a banker.
Maybe I'm something else entirely.
Maybe.

San Diego Swap Meet

All Elvis on one table,
antique fishing reels on another,
blazing turquoise,
brass buckles,
knives,
old-time photos—
but it is the people
who interest me,
trying to make a few dollars
sitting all day
in a Sports Arena lot,
kind,
patient,
smiling,
petting small dogs,
eternally ready for conversation
about anything,
so unlike bankers
I heard testify
before Congress.

The Dream of Greece, Wisconsin, and One-armed Trees

Our governments cut back trees to one branch
so we don't waste fruit on people and birds who can't pay for it.

Along with each branch there is a ribbon-cutting ceremony
for a federally funded tire swing
to keep the unemployed and their children happy.

Greek leaders say Greece is the birthplace
of a free and open democracy.

Wisconsin leaders say each raised fruit at the tip
is a torch in the hand of the Statue of Liberty.

Socrates says to never trust a politician.

In both Greece and Wisconsin, the common man is
an anchovy in a school of barracudas.

Somewhere in the night, a ball game is playing
on a laundromat TV
with two outs and two strikes in the bottom of the ninth.

If Washington Were Pompeii

stone penises carved in sidewalks
erecting their way to ancient brothels
would continue to 1600 Pennsylvania Avenue NW
and the Bush White House,
showing excavators how citizens of a
storybook nation were,
well, you know, fucked.

Before You Were Born

some computer figured
how many bottles of Pepsi
you'd buy
before you died,

how many times you'd make love,
throw dice,
eat crackers.

How many reruns
you'd watch
and watch again.

It wasn't counting
on you waking up, ever.

After 2008

Did you ever stop to think
some crosswalk buttons
you push each day
are connected to nothing?

You push and wait
longer than seems right,
musing maybe the universe
is teaching you patience.

Then one day you experiment
by not using the button
and discover time between signals
is almost the same.

This makes you question
if they were designed by social engineers
instead of electrical engineers,
and similarly, if we are all

being played
so that some day
40 years of your hard labor
in savings and pension

will disappear from banks
the instant symbol makers decide.

Patient Y

says he's scared of continental drift,
that some morning he'll be thrown
from his bed when North America
slams into Europe.

I do my best not to laugh
because his onion face is so serious.
"You really think
that will happen soon?" I ask.

He coldly says he doesn't know,
that he wasn't supposed to lose
his job, house, or wife
of 35 years either.

Demon Fish

After weeks speaking with a homeless man
on my daily walks along the sea

I offer this angler
a ten for a fish story.

He has false starts
until the demon strangles him,

and utterly defeated,
wants to give it back.

I am stunned by his honor
versus lack of it

in White House men
who in 2008 took everything.

Hiking Superstition Mountains I Realized

Oxygen is plant breath.
Paper is tree flesh.
Money is belief.
And no matter
what they say,
America is still
a stolen country.

The Day I Appeared on TV

There was a power outage and the screen went blank
then presto, for the first time, I was in it.

I smiled and a face smiled back.

I raised my arm and an arm lifted.

The sun went behind some clouds
and the spell was broken.

Some say the desert in August does strange things.

I say the next day I gave up television
and went outside.

The Kid at Calico Rock

Listening to the stringy kid
with the acoustic guitar,
I know his wildness of spirit
is stronger than empty pockets
and years of eating canned food.

Maybe the kid worked all summer
washing dishes to buy that guitar.
Maybe he loves it more
than boys on the hill
love their dogs.

They say the place he's from
has a river so polluted
it caught fire.

Hiking the Coast Range Mountains

Life is not
what I thought

Death is not
what I thought

God is not
what I thought

Beside the brook
there is outrageous
laughter

Fishing Trip on the Deschutes River in Oregon

"When it happens,
and it will happen,
you won't see it on TV
or hear it on the radio"
says the lunatic fisherman
in marsh grass
of Central Oregon.

"Osprey will carry trout
and river otters make tracks
like they always have," he says.

His pale blue eyes stare
at my fly rod
then glance into my soul.

He shakes my wrist, saying
"Petroglyphic butterflies
have a right to take flight,
to declare above all
Industrial Oz is not God
and never was."

Then he is gone
and there is only
waiting river.

How to Fish the Wind

You start by listening 40 years
so it can put you through enough
to see if you are worthy
of what it has to say.

Most people can't listen that long
so they have to get the message
second hand from trees.

Reflections on Sand Creek, Colorado

"After the massacre, Soule, the son of abolitionists, wrote letters to his superiors exposing the horror in wrenching detail — fetuses ripped from mothers and scalped, scrotums turned into tobacco pouches, children shot for sport."
— "Hero of Sand Creek Massacre in Colorado honored on 150th anniversary" by David Kelly, *latimes.com*, December 6, 2014

White is the color we flew
that was supposed to protect us
and didn't.

Red is the color of our blood –
children, women, men, and old ones
running from militia volunteers' bullets.

Blue is the color of frozen corpses
left for winter coyotes.

Each time I see a flag
waving in someone's yard
I remember.

People on 17th Street in Portland, Oregon, Dreaming of Dogs

I'm at a potluck block party
listening to a black-haired 30-ish single mom
discussing her dream of rotweilers
chewing red striped pieces of cloth

when another single mom says she too
has been dreaming of dogs,
only these are tiny irate poodles
barking indecipherably into microphones.

The lad who works in the bookstore
says for him it has been St. Bernards
appearing in blizzards, but as he touches them
they flash into skeletons.

No one mentions the war.

View of Modern War from Space Station

In the dream of drinking tea with chopsticks in microgravity
aboard the International Space Station,
Mark reads Homer's *Iliad*, while three astronauts watch real war
like another bout of Ultimate Fighting Championship
but much more serious, of course,
with space-generals placing bets on teams like Fantasy Football
as a group of young men journeys to kill
another group with different uniforms and flag
in elaborate maneuvers
like a sort of death dance, or sun dance, or sun drowning
involving ships, planes, missiles, infantry and tanks
where ants protect an anthill
or a yellow lab barks at his reflection
pawing and snarling back
in a hidden lake
so that up close, when bullet enters human flesh
of his or his enemy's uniform,
and grinding teeth torment the vanquished,
seeded in victor to sprout later,
and facial expression becomes more real
that it ever has been or will be again,
and ordinary life is most valued as it slowly fades,
and dog's nose finally touches water,
the whole illusion shatters.

The Vagrant Says

I live on a deserted island in my mind.
I write novels on gum wrappers
then read them aloud and pretend
I am not the author.
I sleep under a beached sailboat.
I give myself awards
then criticize the awards.
I teach Greek to goldfish.
In truth, I am my only editor,
publisher and audience.
I have the most fun
berating all of the above.
Of course, I talk to myself
and my gibberish has patterns
of lost loves,
a boy soldier in Laos,
war scenes on the Mekong River Delta,
or what could have been
had I held mindfulness
instead of a grenade.

Sometime before I die
I will line up coconuts
against the shed
with my rifle
then sit down
and read to them like children.

Earth Like the Deck of a Ship

Inuits say the sun's position has moved
and tongue drifts changed from north wind
to east wind. That is the real news.

This reminds me of the Luiseno Legend
"Before This Land" about when
"darkness and storms descended"
[. . . .] and "Uu-yot led his people to higher ground
and all were saved"*

or talking to a 2000-year-old insect-and-
fire-resistant redwood
just before sunset near Crescent City
about her view of blue planet homo sapiens

or an old timer who said
"Maybe there is a spaceship you navigate
with an electric guitar.
In the 60s we made songs like that."

*http://indigenouspeople.net/thisland.htm

What I Can't Say at My Neighbor's Party Looking at a Map of the United States

Texas is, and always has always been,
an upside down shark eating Mexico.
Florida is a phallic reminder of how
the nation got screwed – twice.
And who can forget Louisiana
getting the boot during Katrina
with all those families on roofs?

I lived in California during Enron deregulation
where code names "Fat Boy. Death Star. Get Shorty"
made us the laughingstock of the nation,
and for those with no air conditioning in August,
we were a giant handle connected to
everything in this country, and nothing.

I recalled Our Lady of Guadalupe School
in Hermosa Beach where
it was "one nation under God
with liberty and justice for all"
while the flag flapped
it's red star and brown bear.

No one said anything about Mexican families
dying of thirst or hypothermia
in the Sonoran and Chihuahuan Deserts,
and mountain areas, trying anything
to get across the border.
Instead, all eyes were fixed on Christ,
white as Wonder Bread with its red,
yellow, and blue balloons
like crayons melting into Redondo's Saltwater Pool,
or we stared at the mighty Pacific
with her bikinis, surfboards, and steel-blue fish.

Ode to a Mexican Family

The day San Diego radio reported
attempts to save the cross
on Mt. Soledad

was the day it reported
burning of migrant camps
in McGonigle Canyon.

The announcer read both
like ingredients for bread.

Intoxicated by Purple Lupine,

curved alders are mastodon tusks
and Budweisers bloom on hillsides.

Red-helmeted river rafters march
like the Chinese Army.

You could say this is a poem
about mastodons or drunks

or even prophecy.
One can hope when government drunks

and the Federal Reserve lose what remains
of our country to China,

and our sacred Constitution
and institutions are gone like mastodon,

these purple lupine will remain.

Creative Writing Professor as Iron Worker

Yes, iron-thought makes bombs.
But if you keep it in the fire long enough,
it can also be a river the color of flowers
that can be shaped, while hot,
into anything you want or need
to get through your days.
Dostoevsky. Tolstoy.
The Diary of Anne Frank.

For writers, this sweating, dangerous,
ancient work
lets you and others know,
in spite of everything
wrong in our difficult world,
among rusted flywheels,
screw drivers, pipe wrenches,
junkyard wrecked machinery,
something more human was here.

Local History

Mother Teresa works at the Post Office.

Hitler works at the bank.

Che has a new gig
as a Poet in the Schools.

Sakharov, who worked at the Pentagon,
now helps an NGO in Iraq.

Of course these names are labels
for others

whose energies swirl
at the edge of a shared dream –

history, experience, reality
all the universe's way of saying

right here, in this moment,
choose.

Another Legend of Stonehenge

When our people were dying
from the invaders

our souls went into the deer
and when the deer were killed

our souls went into the fish
and when the fish were killed

our souls went into the spruce
and when the spruce were killed

we went into these stones
which could not be killed.

After Two Weeks in Wilderness

I hate my car's metal skin,
dinosaur eyes,
dinosaur blood,
exhaust breath,
driven through darkness
by something
that passes
for human.

God Doesn't Show Up at Rose Festival Parade

Instead, in the form of a sparrow,
He visits an alley vet with PTSD.

Princesses go by waving like wind-up toys.
There are too many balloons and flowers to count.

Soon, everyone will go home to their TVs
and leave him alone,

except this one sparrow that for some reason
all night keeps coming back.

The Fishes He Caught

The fishes he caught
had faces of dead pilgrims.
They had arrowhead fins
and their eyes glowed
like coals on foggy nights.

They spoke in unknown tongues
like human voices
around distant campfires.

Their scales reflected silver coins
dropped in pond water, each with
the silhouette of a hanged man.

That night he dreamed of trout fishing
on his father's lake
he caught these strange beasts
one after another.

He had no clue what they wanted
or why they took his bait.

Enlightenment for $19.99

"Seeing a whale in your dream represents your intuition and awareness. You are in tuned to your sense of spirituality. Alternatively, it indicates a relationship or business project that is too enormous to handle."
— *Dream Dictionary* at HYPERDICTIONARY.COM

said the ad in the dream
so I sent a check but the big E never arrived

just like BAZOOKA Bubble Gum's
genuine whale tooth

I'm still waiting 45 years for
and which both the dream

and real Post Office clerks
are unable to track

even though I still recall BAZOOKA at
Box 9200, St. Paul, MINN 55177.

The dream librarian says
the E ad never existed

but the whale tooth ad did
until sometime in 70s

Minnesota ran out of whales
or international treaties blocked access,

and the green, red, black, and gray wrapper did say
"NOT VALID WHERE PROHIBITED,

REGULATED OR TAXED"
and maybe Hermosa Beach was.

Anyway, says my dream therapist,
the whale tooth was a Jungian symbol

for "awareness […or] a relationship
that is too […big] to handle"

so the dream-real-tooth will cause immense pain
until I flee what is biting me

or I get a giant spiritual toothbrush
or do battle with a giant symbolic squid.

"And," she adds,
"the Big E would be a bargain

if it could be bought at any price
except transcendence and grief, but it can't."

Peter Went Fishing

The Master said to throw in a hook and line,
then to remove a coin from the mouth of the first fish.
He didn't say anything about a game warden.

"So let me get this straight, young man.
Your 'Master' told you to get a coin
from the mouth of a fish. How exactly does that work?"

"Well, I don't know," Peter replied, undaunted.
"But you can watch."

"Nope," said the warden. "You can't even cast
without a proper fishing license."

Peter returned skunked.
"Where's the coin?" asked the Master.

"A game warden said I would get a ticket."

"I sent him too," said the Master.
"Who has more weight with you?"

Ancient Sacred Texts Conversing in the Library at Alexandria

That camel herder is learning
to *Make a Million Deben*

while his son reads
50 Ways to Seduce Women.

Near the bay window
one reads *Cleopatra's Beauty Secrets*

as if inner beauty doesn't exist.
These people have Sappho

and the universe at their fingertips
but they don't care.

They'd rather read the usual goat skins.

Poem Against Yellow School Buses

Someday, they will be green and blue as the Earth,
not social-conditioning yellow like yield signs.

The first thing a child sees in the Oregon morning
should be hope, not an overripe banana on wheels.

School boards will resist, of course, with cries
of "tradition, consistency, accident prevention"

but there are other planetary concerns
real as rain, or the lack thereof.

Techno Man

with all the people skills of a carp
says it is not logically possible
I caught a virus from my computer.

"Oh yeah?" I tell him,
"someone sneezed on my keyboard."
He says that doesn't count.

I ask who made him the authority
on what does and doesn't count,
and he says the question is irrelevant,

but I can request an antimicrobial keyboard
from the supply room
if it's important to me.

I tell him instead of Microsoft Windows®
I want a real window
where I can see birds in flight.

Unintended Art

Most wanted to be part
of the conversation
so they were,
but very few were part
of *the* conversation.

A painted-over cricket
on stucco
is beautiful
only so long
before you want
to hear his song.

On the Ferry Between Port Angeles and Victoria

Someday there will be
no sign humans existed,

settled in coves
after an ice age,

plowed squares
for boxes to live in,

made art, reservoirs
or weapons.

But yesterday,
I gave a five

to a Native woman
holding cardboard

who smiled
like the red ball sun—

almost too bright
to look at.

Poem for Ishi

Imagine being the last survivor
of the United States of America,

your people bounty-hunted
by invaders from across the sea

at 25 cents a scalp
and five dollars a head,

you, hiding in a barn, hungry,
thinking of your murdered father,

mother and sister's winter supplies
taken as souvenirs by land surveyors

yet you never give up on God
or ancestral dreams,

but later, reflecting on your role
as a pneumonic museum piece

in what the Yelamu called Chutchui
before it was Berkeley, CA,

recall years before Kroeber
took you in to study,

how, as a boy
among wild poppies,

crimson was a beautiful color.

Inspired by the film *Ishi, the Last Yahi* available at jedriffefilms.com

Houses on Siletz Spit

"Sawed logs within the spit indicate that the portion of the Siletz Spit on which the houses had been built must have suffered previous erosion, sometime after 1895. After that early erosion the dunes must have built back out and become re-established."
— *The Causes of Erosion to Siletz Spit, Oregon*, by Paul D. Komar and C. Cary Rea, Oregon State University Sea Grant College Program, 1975.

Every hundred years or so
the river swells like a sea
and crazy happens –

driftwood in living rooms,
underwater saltwater kitchens,
docks and moorages swept away.

Old ones' homes are dry
on upriver stilts
while new construction is gone

as if it never existed
until the next owners
and those who would cheat them

arrive from the east.
Gary at Coyote Rock told me
this would happen

to anyone who didn't listen
to men who have dwelled here
ten thousand years.

Coyote's Prediction

There is a ghost
like water healing
river's paddle wounds,

old logging mill
lanced by seeds
of forgotten giants,

salmon cannery
weathered like ribs
of a fish skeleton.

Only things
that belong here
will last.

Congress of Fish

Salmon will eat herring and squid.
Herring and squid get smaller fish.
Smaller fish get krill.
Krill get phytoplankton.
Phytoplankton get sunlight.

And gill-slit moonfish
in womb of his mother
on tanning bed
gets to destroy everything.

Big Sur Satori

The pod of gray whales
spouting off Hearst Castle
probably thought –
whatever.

Crows and squirrels over
a "No Trespassing" sign
probably thought –
whatever.

If my civilization drives
off a cliff into
uncountable stars
many probably think

whatever.

River Reflections

Like the elk
my vote
won't be heard.

I have little
economic
or political power.

I'm uninterested
in matters
lacking soul.

I gave up
television
when I was 15.

I am a nonessential
and unproductive
worker

yet a threat
to the machine
merely by resting

and thinking.

At Lake Absarraca

a homeless man
tells me to keep fluoride
out of my Christianity,
or, in other words,
don't judge him

while another claims
cell towers
are brain forks.

They both
may be right.

On the grassy plain
outside Cheyenne
formerly caged
buffalo and elk
are gone,
and I imagine
something in men
who freed them
was also set free.

Bear-like Tree Shadows
on a Dying Chinook Salmon

I saw a wind storm in the Nehalem forest
with story clouds in shapes of villages
rolling in from the Pacific
and heard a voice, not fish and not human
but told in river reflections
of an elder fish whom, to understand bear,
became one so completely in his dream
there was a chance he couldn't return
to being salmon here either,
and so the legend goes about a grizzly fish
lying in shallows with gills and a dorsal fin,
about his mistake not being rooted in himself
enough, at first, to resist
the lure of voices around him,
as a spirit sometimes becomes a man
and also forgets.

Raft Trip

My friend says five ranchers near Klamath Falls
shot themselves when water was cut.

"Their families were promised water into perpetuity
as a condition for settling here in the 1800s."

He adds, "I know you used to work for Greenpeace
and think water is for salmon."

"Tell me more," I offer, imaging myself with a gun.
"I knew them," he says. "They were all good men."

Looking at Mr. Steelhead in our raft,
I think of 30,000 salmon, mostly chinook, that died in 2002

from suffocation and disease brought by drought.
I think of these five men at the end,

one in a room upstairs looking at photos of better days,
another scanning his land thinking about children and grandchildren.

A third reading Marquez's *One Hundred Years of Solitude:*
"Many years later, as he faced the firing squad,

Colonel Aureliano Buendía was to remember that distant
afternoon when his father took him to discover ice."

Floating on summer silence, casting below alders,
I say "We have to do better for ranchers and salmon."

and think, but don't say, it will take uncommon vision,
sacrifice, and planning this world has never seen.

If

Miami and Manhattan will be underwater,

Tulsa and Omaha sport surfaces like Mars,

North American animals become mere animations

on a silver screen,

money becomes worthless,

the young and vital stop being tools

for the old and fat,

Norway's seed bank is

the new Fort Knox,

what shall we write, sing, paint

and *What Shall I Put in the Hole That I Dig?**

*Children's book by by Eleanor Thompson (Author), Aliki (Illustrator)

Octomato Nightmare

"A common claim made by this group is that GM foods have been proved safe to eat and that there is a global scientific consensus to support this statement; therefore, no labeling is needed. However, an examination of the scientific data, along with discussions on this topic in other countries, show that both claims are blatantly false."
— David Schubert of the Salk Institute for Biological Studies, "Why we need GMO labels," *cnn.com*, updated February 3, 2014 (Salk Institute for Biological Studies was ranked number 1 in the United States for Neuroscience & Behavior, 1998-2008, by sciencewatch.com)

"[. . .] skeptics have focused on research conducted by DNA Plant Technology, a company that developed an experimental, genetically engineered tomato in 1991. The tomato included a modified gene from a breed of arctic flounder that, it was hoped, would allow the tomatoes to be more resistant to frost and cold storage."
— pbs.org, "Genetically Modified Tomatoes" at *DNA. Hot Science. Gallery of Genetic Modifications*

The Law of Unintended Consequences meant instead of resisting frost
perhaps tomatoes were finned and spotted, and wouldn't sell
with discounted bananas on fruit and vegetable racks.

This playing with DNA reminds me of a river kid
who claimed people in his town had woolly hair
because of sheep intestine condoms. Not scientific, but . . .

Maybe those who eat octopus-flavored hybrids
will have grandkids needing 3 handlebars,
or 4, or 5, or even 8 on tricycles. Maybe not.

But who wants to take the risk to save 29¢ a pound
when Vermont and all of Europe, Brazil, Russia,
Japan, China, Australia – 64 countries in total – require labeling?

Corporate scientists will say consumers' worst nightmare
come true is "an evolutionary feature instead of a bug": "Those extra
limbs are great for basketball guards and defensive linebackers."

In a *USA Today* article in the year 2084, what won't be reported,
if Monsanto gets it way, will be superhero athletes
turning purple-red when angry and squirting ink out their butts.

Saint Arkhipov

"It is certain that Arkhipov's reputation was a key factor in the control room debate. The previous year the young officer had exposed himself to severe radiation in order to save a submarine with an overheating reactor."
— "Thank you Vasili Arkhipov, the man who stopped nuclear war" by Edward Wilson, *The Guardian*, October 27, 2012

That day in the sub
the vote was 2 to 1 to launch
a nuclear torpedo
at carrier *USS Randolf*

but Officer Vasili Arkhipov
single-handedly
stopped it
refusing to fear WWIII.

I was 27 days and nights
from surfacing
out of my mother
and owe him my life.

Later, before I read
Tolstoy, Chekhov,
Solzhenitsyn, Sakharov,
Dostoyevsky,

instead of honoring
the peasant turned captain,
I hated Russians
in President Reagan's

"Evil Empire" speech
which reminded me of
"duck and cover"
below my first grade desk

at Our Lady of Guadalupe
where I imagined
being vaporized
as a firecrackered figurine

of an unknown saint.

Instead of Drones, I Dream of Peace Piñatas

"It was a wonderful feeling to be delivering food and help, rather than delivering bombs [...] In the beginning of the candy drops, Halverson used his own weekly candy ration. Soon the other pilots and support staff started giving their candy and gum and their handkerchiefs. The project grew so big that his old [Army] base also began to contribute candy and handkerchiefs."
— *trumanlibrary.org*

Make drones the size of Goodyear Blimps,
showering dried fruit,
seeds, and poems
over the so-called enemy

showing even in a crisis
we are people too,
making commanders report
numbers smiling

instead of numbers killed,
piñatas like a cloud race
of fat medieval dragons
across the Earth,

citizens everywhere
growing gardens
for the war effort.
Anything to forget

the other two dragon bombs
Truman dropped.

Advisory

I tell Mom the apricot jam tastes wrong
and I need to see the jar.
It says "Best by June 1973."
It is April 2010.
I dig and discover Tylenol expired 1976,
other jams 1978 and 1981.

"Scott, you can't pay attention to all that,"
she offers, like a fly landed on a paper plate
at an Oregon picnic.
"Those dates are merely advisory.
Besides, the print is too small."

By next Thanksgiving,
I bought her a magnifying glass
but the problem remains.
"I don't like using it," she says.
"If it bothers you so much,
you read the labels."

Going through her pantry
and medicine cabinets,
tossing bags of expired items,
I recall sandstone wheel ruts
in Guernsey, Wyoming,
on what was the Oregon Trail,
hardy souls like Mom
stubborn as Montana salmon,
who refused to listen to anyone
on the long path back
to a new/old country.

Three-Sided Lizard

Driving south on I-5, it looks like a place for jobs.

From the other direction, it provides goods and services.

Everyone knows its guts are poisoning the Earth

and may kill us all in the end

but the Supreme Court ruled

that lizard is a person

who can only be jailed on paper

in which case the Lizard God

will merely print more paper

like in 2009.

Facts

The sun does not rise,
has never risen.
Instead the Earth turns.

In the same way
you and I are not the
center.

Reality is an ox
carrying a red dotted
purple balloon

in her jaw that says
this place, so unlike all others,
is "Not for sale."

"State OKs money for drone test range in Eastern Oregon" – KATU.com, 3/22/15

Imagine a drone takes out a fisherman "for practice" because
"There wasn't nothing else to shoot at.
The deer move too fast, and rams blend into the landscape."

His fishing buddies, none too happy, shoot back
as drones fall for months like clay pigeons.

So drones move to the coast where they take out more fishermen.
"Well, hell," says the Drone supervisor. "There are too damn many
fishermen in Oregon anyway. Get a few. Protect the resource."

Sounds strange, right? But not half as strange as the secret Green Run
that in 1949 intentionally doused nearby U. S. citizens with radiation.

Or, Captain Kermit Beahan, who bombed Nagasaki, answering
a question about his "most outstanding experience on this historic flight."
"I suppose it was when the clouds opened up over the target…
pretty as a picture. I made the run, let the bomb go. That was my greatest thrill."
as 40, 000 burned to death, and skin peeled off screaming children
while maybe he went back for a beer.

Or Ret. Adm. Eugene Carroll, USN, complaining, "When I was finally assigned
a target in central Europe that had marginal military value
but I was supposed to destroy that target [if ordered]…
If I had done that…I would have killed 600,000 people…"

Thoughts like this turning over stones for nymphs and midges
whenever fishin's slow.

Salish Sea Prophecy

Many years after no fish, men kept fishing
like a yellow lab paws a carpet
or a black-tailed deer crashes into a fence.

Someone reported a silver flash in a creek
that turned out to be a Virginia license plate
from days anyone could drive.

Rock shadows or pieces of logs
took shapes of dorsals and tails
but only in men's minds.

Ancestors had it all – snowy Thunderbird Mountains,
vast mysterious sea, uncountable salmon
returning each spring and fall.

Now there are only stories of those days,
and men who still believe
they and their green god know better.

Forget Math and English

What I recall from grade school
was a 747 with a kick start,
chicken with lips,
submarine with a screen door,
snake with armpits

all preparing me for
a President with honesty,
and news that risks truth.

Snowflake Immortality

Gazing across
this wide valley
it's hard to imagine
each flake's different,
same snow,
same cold,
same beauty,
same sea.

Acknowledgments

Grateful acknowledgment is made to the following publications or shows in which these poems first appeared or are forthcoming.

The 2River View: "The Kid at Calico Rock"

About Place Journal: "Meteor" *Afterthoughts* (Canada): "Erratum"

Amsterdam Quarterly: "At Lake Absarraca," "Of Whales and the Hinckley Hunt on Christmas Eve, 1818"

Artists' Milepost Art Show, Unnatural Acts: Crimes Against Mother Nature: Antarctic Dream After Watching Chasing Ice" (Portland, November 2013)

Bathyspheric Review: "Smoked Whale, Circa 1987"

Blast Furnace: "Antarctic Dream After Watching Chasing Ice"

Blood Orange Review: "The Fishes He Caught"

Blue Lotus Review: "Hiking the Superstition Mountains I Realized", "Intoxicated by Purple Lupine"

Canary: "Coyote's Prediction," "Men Wandering Around Alaska Looking for a TV Set"

Carbon Culture Review: "Techno Man"

Cascadia Review: "Speaking to a Street Person About the Problem With North America"

Cement Squeeze: "Plutonium Fish"

Chaos Poetry Review: "Demon Fish"

Clementine Poetry Journal: "Wasting Sea Stars"

Cobra Lily: "Earth Like the Deck of a Ship"

Confrontation: "View of Modern War from Space Station"

Cream City Review: "The Dream of Greece, Wisconsin, and One-armed Trees"

Festival Writer: "Enlightenment for $19.99"

The Fieldstone Review: "Houses on Siletz Spit"

Flycatcher: "Big Sur Satori," "Omen Poem"
The Foster Collective's Landslide Gallery Show, "Gulf Oil Disaster Response" (Chicago, July/August 2010), which featured art and words on gas station paper towels: "Louisiana Agates"

Green Fuse: "At the Nevada Nuclear Test Site" (published under the title "At the Nuclear Test Site")
Hermes Poetry Journal: "Forget Math and English"

Hubbub: "People on 17th Street in Portland, Oregon, Dreaming of Dogs" (published under the title "People on 17th Street Dreaming of Dogs")

The Kerf: "In Oracle, Arizona," "Rain Forest Poem"

Lake: a Journal of Arts and Environment Web site (Canada): "After Two Weeks in Wilderness"

The Lucid Stone: "Men Wandering Around Alaska Looking for a TV Set" (published under the title "Men Wandering Around Heaven Looking for a TV Set"

Mandrake Poetry Review (Poland): "Snowflake Immortality"

Mr. Cogito: "Coyote's Prediction"

Moksha Journal: "Before You Were Born"

The Monarch Review: "Thinking About AWP 2014 in Seattle"

MOSS (mosszine.com): "Glacial River Poem"

Niche Magazine: "Patient Y"

The Nisqually Delta Review: "Another Legend of Stonehenge," "Thinking About Global Warming and the Orange Tree Outside My Kitchen Window"

The November 3rd Club: "If Washington Were Pompeii"

OccuPoetry: "Listening to a Banker Talk About Losing [Only] Two Billion Dollars as Schools Are Closed," "San Diego Swap Meet"

Pacific Call: "Listening to Fireworks Near the 2014 FOR Seabeck Conference," "Wrecking Ball Dream"

Pemmican: "Moon and Money Poem"

Poetry 24: "*Essex*, 1820"

Poets for Living Waters: "Louisiana Agates"

Rain: "Bear-like Tree Shadows on a Dying Chinook Salmon," "The Old One's Letter"

The Raven Chronicles: "Hiking the Coast Range Mountains" (published under the title "Hiking the Coast Range")

rfishc.com: "Photo Circa 1969, The Art of Redaction"

Rivet: The Journal of Writing That Risks: "What I Can't Say at My Neighbor's Party Looking at a Map of the United States"

San Diego Poetry Annual 2014 - 2015: "The Vagrant Says"

Shark Reef: "Poem for Ishi"

Slipsteam, Poems and Other Currents (Blog) by Kristin Berger: "How to Fish the Wind"

South 85: "On the Ferry Between Port Angeles and Victoria"

South Ash Press: "Reflections in a Garden of Undersea Statues" (published under the title "Reflections in a Garden of Statues")

Split Rock Review: "Bumper Sticker: Extinction is Forever," "Otter Log"

Teaching English in the Two-Year College (TETYC): "Creative Writing Professor as Iron Worker"

Tidal Basin Review: "Salish Sea Poem"

The Trumpeter: Journal of Ecosophy (Canada): "Brook Trout"

Two Hawks Quarterly: "After 2008"

Untitled Country Review: "Ancient Sacred Texts Conversing in the Library at Alexandria," "How to Fish the Wind"

Wild Earth: "And They Thought We Were Talking About Caribou"

"Bear-like Tree Shadows on a Dying Chinook Salmon," "Glacial River Poem," "How to Fish the Wind," and "Photo Circa 1969, The Art of Redaction" appeared in the chapbook *River Walker* by Mountains and Rivers Press.
"At the Nevada Nuclear Test Site" (published under the title "At the Nuclear Test Site"), "Coyote's Prediction," "Erratum," "The Kid

at Calico Rock," "Plutonium Fish," and "Through a Wire Fence" appeared in the chapbook *The Eyes of Those Who Broke Free* by Pudding House Publications.

"And They Thought We Were Talking About Caribou," "Antarctic Dream After Watching *Chasing Ice,*" "Before You Were Born," "The Dream of Greece, Wisconsin, and One-armed Trees," "Hiking the Superstitions I Realized," "How It Is," "Listening to a Banker Talk About Losing [Only] Two Billion Dollars as Schools Are Closed," "Louisiana Agates," "Moon and Money Poem," "On the Ferry Between Port Angeles and Victoria," "Patient Y," "Poem Against Yellow School Buses," "River Reflections," "San Diego Swap Meet," "Thinking About Global Warming and the Orange Tree Outside My Kitchen Window," "What If One Night a Highly Charged Comet Went By," and "Why All US-Made Nuclear Waste Must Be Stored at the White House" appeared in the chapbook *The Other History . . .* by FutureCycle Press.

"After Two Weeks in Wilderness," "Another Legend of Stonehenge," "Brook Trout," "The Day I Appeared on TV," "The Fishes He Caught," "Fishing Trip on the Deschutes River in Oregon," "Hiking the Coast Range Mountains," "If Washington Were Pompeii," "The Kid at Calico Rock," "Men Wandering Around Alaska Looking for a TV Set," "People on 17th Street in Portland, Oregon, Dreaming of Dogs," "Reflections on Sand Creek, Colorado," "River Reflections," and "Smoked Whale, Circa 1987" appeared in the chapbook *The Warrior Poems* by Pudding House Publications.

"Coyote's Prediction" and "Plutonium Fish" appeared in the anthology *Fresh Water: Poems from the Rivers, Lakes, and Streams* by Pudding House Publications.

Thanks to Artsmith on Orcas Island for a 2013 residency fellowship which allowed me to work on these poems.

Fomite

A fomite is a medium capable of transmitting infectious organisms from one individual to another.

"The activity of art is based on the capacity of people to be infected by the feelings of others." Tolstoy, *What Is Art?*

Writing a review on Amazon, Good Reads, Shelfari, Library Thing or other social media sites for readers will help the progress of independent publishing. To submit a review, go to the book page on any of the sites and follow the links for reviews. Books from independent presses rely on reader to reader communications.

For more information or to order any of our books, visit
http://www.fomitepress.com/FOMITE/Our_Books.html

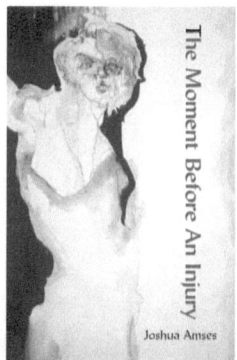

The Moment Before an Injury
Joshua Amses

Nothing Beside Remains
Jaysinh Birjépatil

The Way None of This Happened
Mike Breiner

Cycling in Plato's Cave
David Cavanagh

Victor Rand
David Brizer

Summer on the Cold War Planet
Paula Closson Buck

Fomite

Picking Up the Bodies
James F. Connolly

Unfinished Stories of Girls
Catherine Zobal Dent

Drawing on Life
Mason Drukman

Foreign Tales of
Exemplum and Woe
J. C. Ellefson

Free Fall/Caída libre
Tina Escaja

Sinfonia Bulgarica
Zdravka Evtimova

Derail Thie Train Wreck
Daniel Forbes

Where There Are Two or More
Elizabeth Genovise

The Hundred Yard Dash Man
Barry Goldensohn

Fomite

When You Remeber
Deir Yassin
R. L. Green

In A Family Way
Zeke Jarvis

A Guide
to the Western Slopes
Roger Lebovitz

Confessions of a Carnivore
Diane Lefer

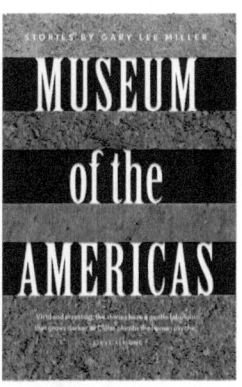

Museum of the Americas
Gary Lee Miller

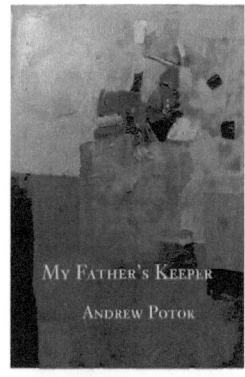

My Father's Keeper
Andrew Potok

The Hole That Runs
Through Utopia
Joseph D. Reich

Companion Plants
Kathryn Roberts

Rafi's World
Fred Russell

Fomite

My Murder and Other Local News
David Schein

Bread & Sentences
Peter Schumann

Principles of Navigation
Lynn Sloan

Among Angelic Orders
Susan Thoma

Everyone Lives Here
Sharon Webster

The Falkland Quartet
Tony Whedon

The Return of Jason Green
Suzi Wizowaty

The Inconveniece of the Wings
Silas Dent Zobal

Fomite

More Titles from Fomite...

Joshua Amses — *Raven or Crow*
Joshua Amses — *The Moment Before an Injury*
Jaysinh Birjepatil — *The Good Muslim of Jackson Heights*
Antonello Borra — *Alfabestiario*
Antonello Borra — *AlphaBetaBestiario*
Jay Boyer — *Flight*
Dan Chodorkoff — *Loisada*
Michael Cocchiarale — *Still Time*
Greg Delanty — *Loosestrife*
Zdravka Evtimova — *Carts and Other Stories*
Anna Faktorovich — *Improvisational Arguments*
Derek Furr — *Suite for Three Voices*
Stephen Goldberg — *Screwed*
Barry Goldensohn — *The Listener Aspires to the Condition of Music*
Greg Guma — *Dons of Time*
Andrei Guruianu — *Body of Work*
Ron Jacobs — *The Co-Conspirator's Tale*
Ron Jacobs — *Short Order Frame Up*
Ron Jacobs — *All the Sinners Saints*
Kate MaGill — *Roadworthy Creature, Roadworthy Craft*
Ilan Mochari — *Zinsky the Obscure*
Jennifer Moses — *Visiting Hours*
Sherry Olson — *Four-Way Stop*
Janice Miller Potter — *Meanwell*
Jack Pulaski — *Love's Labours*
Charles Rafferty — *Saturday Night at Magellan's*

Fomite

Joseph D. Reich — *The Derivation of Cowboys & Indians*
Joseph D. Reich — *The Housing Market*
Fred Russell — *Rafi's World*
Peter Schumann — *Planet Kasper, Volume 1*
L. E. Smith — *The Consequence of Gesture*
L. E. Smith — *Travers' Inferno*
L. E. Smith — *Views Cost Extra*
Susan Thomas — *The Empty Notebook Interrogates Itself*
Tom Walker — *Signed Confessions*
Susan V. Weiss — *My God, What Have We Done?*
Peter Mathiessen Wheelwright — *As It Is On Earth*

www.ingramcontent.com/pod-product-compliance
Lightning Source LLC
Chambersburg PA
CBHW021442080526
44588CB00009B/645